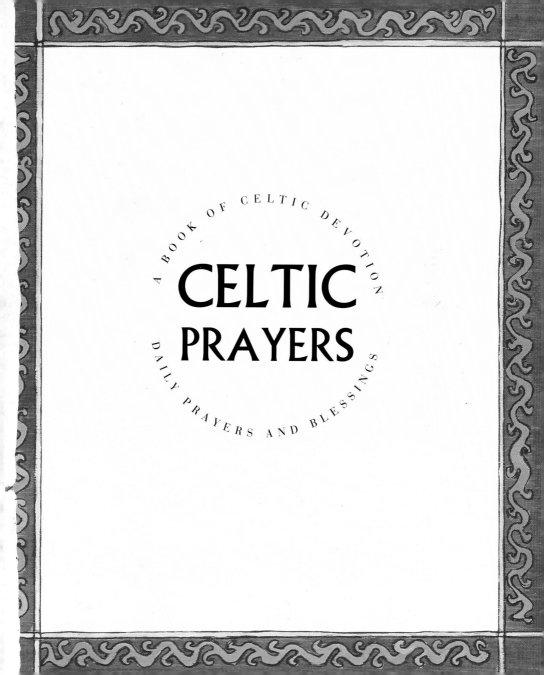

CELTIC PRAYERS

A BOOK OF CELTIC DEVOTION

DAILY PRAYERS AND BLESSINGS

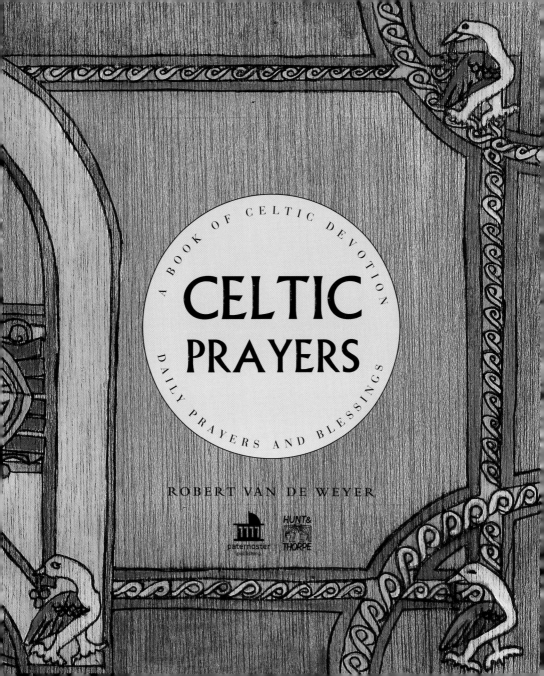

A BOOK OF CELTIC DEVOTION

CELTIC
PRAYERS

DAILY PRAYERS AND BLESSINGS

ROBERT VAN DE WEYER

paternoster publishing · HUNT & THORPE

Copyright © 1997 Hunt & Thorpe

Text © 1997 Robert Van de Weyer

ISBN 1-85608-281-4

Designed and produced by
THE BRIDGEWATER BOOK COMPANY LTD.

Write to:
Hunt & Thorpe
Laurel House, Station Approach, New Alresford,
Hampshire, SO24 9JH, UK

Hunt & Thorpe is a name used under licence by
Paternoster Publishing, PO Box 300,
Kingstown Broadway, Carlisle, CA3 0QW, UK

A CIP catalog record for this book
is available from the British Library.

Manufactured in Singapore

THE PRAYERS OF THE CELTS

To the Celtic Christians there was no distinction between religion and daily life, no division between the spiritual and the material realms. They perceived the divine spirit in every person, every animal and plant, and in every event. And so their religious faith permeated every aspect of their existence.

The prayers contained in this book reflect the fusion of religion and life. Even the most humdrum and mundane activities merit prayers for God's blessing. And, equally, moments of crisis, or scenes of great beauty, stimulate prayers of intense emotion. For anyone who wishes to follow St. Paul's injunction, to "pray without ceasing," these prayers provide an inspirational model.

The origin of these prayers is obscure, since they have mostly come down to us by word of mouth. They were collected and written down by scholars in the nineteenth century, who visited remote regions of Ireland, Scotland, Wales, and Cornwall, where the old Celtic languages were still spoken. Some prayers may be comparatively recent, but the majority probably date back to the great flowering of Celtic Christianity, initiated by the arrival of

Religion and everyday existence were entwined for the Celtic Christian.

You gave each wind its own color: the north wind is white, bringing snow in winter; the south wind is red, carrying warmth in summer; the west wind is blue, a cooling breeze across the sea; the east wind is yellow, scorching in summer and bitter in winter; and the lesser winds are green, orange, purple and black – the black wind that blows in the darkest nights.

King, you measured each object and each span within the universe: the heights of the mountains and the depths of the oceans; the distance from the sun to the moon, and from star to star.

You ordained the movements of every object: the sun to cross the sky each day, and the moon to rise each night; the clouds to carry rain from the sea, and the rivers to carry water back from the sea.

King, you divided the earth into three zones: the north cold and bitter; the south hot and dry; and the middle zone cool, wet, and fertile.

And you created men and women to be your stewards of the earth, always praising you for your boundless love.

CAEDMON'S HYMN

Now must we praise the Guardian of
heaven,
The might of the Lord and his wisdom of
mind,
The work of the Father of Glory, maker of
all wonders.
He, Holy Creator, first fashioned heaven
As a roof for the sons of men.
Then the eternal Guardian of mankind
Adorned the earth below, a land for men,
Almighty King and everlasting Lord.

A MILLION MIRACLES

O Son of God, perform a miracle for
me: change my heart.
You, whose crimson blood redeems
mankind, whiten my heart.

It is you who makes the sun bright and
the ice sparkle; you who makes the
rivers flow and the salmon leap.

Your skilled hand makes the nut tree
blossom, and the wheat turn golden;
your spirit composes the songs of the
birds and the buzz of the bees.

Your creation is a million wondrous
miracles, beautiful to behold. I ask of
you just one more miracle: beautify my
soul.

TIME

*Take no oath by the earth that you stand
on. You walk on it only for a while, but
soon you shall be buried within it.*

*Pay no heed to the world you live in. You
are dazzled by its pomp and pleasure,
but soon you shall be carried from it.*

*Time is like the ebbing tide on the beach.
You cannot see it move by staring at it,
but soon it has run away from sight.*

*"Time is like the ebbing tide
on the beach."*

2

Sea & Sky

*"I can see the wide ocean, stretching west,
north, and south to the ends of the earth."*

GOD

I am the wind that breathes upon
 the sea,
I am the wave on the ocean,
I am the murmur of leaves rustling,
I am the rays of the sun,
I am the beam of the moon and stars,
I am the power of trees growing,
I am the bud breaking into blossom,
I am the movement of the salmon
 swimming,
I am the courage of the wild boar
 fighting,
I am the speed of the stag running,
I am the strength of the ox pulling
 the plow,
I am the size of the mighty oak tree,
And I am the thoughts of all people
Who praise my beauty and grace.

THE HERMIT IN A CAVE

*As I look out from my cave, I can see the
 wide ocean, stretching west, north, and
 south to the ends of the earth.*

*I watch the sea birds swoop, and I hear
 them shriek; and in my mind I can see
 the ocean depths teeming with fish.*

*The earth is both majestic and playful, both
 solemn and joyful; in all this it reflects
 the One who made it.*

A Tree Oratory

My little oratory gives me greater delight than the finest mansion. From it I can watch the sun and the moon move across the sky, and the stars gather like soldiers to guard me at night.

Who made it? God made it. He planted the seed that grew into this mighty tree. And, where the boughs rise out of the trunk, he fashioned a hollow where I can sit.

Who protects me? God protects me. He put branches and leaves above me to shield me from rain. And he put me high above the ground, safe from the spears and swords of robbers.

Praying with the Spirit

Sometimes when I pray, I utter the words,
But I do not feel or think them.
Sometimes when I pray, I utter the words,
Thinking about what I say, but not feeling.
Sometimes when I pray, I utter the words,
And I both think and feel what I say.

An act of will cannot make me feel,
Nor stop my mind from wandering.
An act of will can only make me utter.
So I shall utter the words,
And let the spirit do the rest,
Guiding my mind and heart as he wills.

"He put branches and leaves above me to shield me from rain."

COLUMBA'S ROCK

Delightful it is to stand on the peak of
a rock, in the bosom of the isle,
gazing on the face of the sea.

I hear the heaving waves chanting a
tune to God in heaven; I see their
glittering surf.

I see the golden beaches; their sands
sparkling; I hear the joyous shrieks
of the swooping gulls.

I hear the waves breaking, crashing on
rocks, like thunder in heaven. I see
the mighty whales.

I watch the ebb and flow of the ocean
tide; it holds my secret, my
mournful flight from Eire.

Contrition fills my heart as I hear the
sea; it chants my sins, sins too
numerous to confess.

Let me bless almighty God, whose
power extends over sea and land,
whose angels watch over all.

Let me study sacred books to calm my
soul; I pray for peace, kneeling at
heaven's gates.

Let me do my daily work, gathering
seaweed, catching fish, giving food
to the poor.

Let me say my daily prayers, sometimes
chanting, sometimes quiet, always
thanking God.

Delightful it is to live on a peaceful
isle, in a quiet cell, serving the King
of kings.

BRENDAN'S PRAYER
BEFORE SETTING SAIL

Shall I abandon, O King of Mysteries, the soft comforts of home? Shall I turn my back on my native land, and my face toward the sea?

Shall I put myself wholly at the mercy of God, without silver, without a horse, without fame and honor? Shall I throw myself wholly on the King of kings, without sword and shield, without food and drink, without a bed to lie on?

Shall I say farewell to my beautiful land, placing myself under Christ's yoke? Shall I pour out my heart to him, confessing my manifold sins and begging forgiveness, tears streaming down my cheeks?

Shall I leave the prints of my knees on the sandy beach, a record of my final prayer in my native land? Shall I then suffer every kind of wound that the sea can inflict?

Shall I take my tiny coracle across the wide, sparkling ocean? O King of the Glorious Heaven, shall I go of my own choice upon the sea?

O Christ, will you help me on the wild waves?

*"Shall I throw myself wholly
on the King of kings?"*

PART TWO

3

DAY & NIGHT

*"Let us go forth… in the gracious
guidance of the angels."*

THE RISING

Let us go forth,
In the goodness of our merciful Father,
In the gentleness of our brother Jesus,
In the radiance of his Holy Spirit,
In the faith of the apostles,
In the joyful praise of the angels,
In the holiness of the saints,
In the courage of the martyrs.

Let us go forth,
In the wisdom of our all-seeing Father,
In the patience of our all-loving brother,
In the truth of the all-knowing Spirit,
In the learning of the apostles,
In the gracious guidance of the angels,
In the patience of the saints,
In the self-control of the martyrs.

Such is the path for all servants of Christ,
The path from death to eternal life.

MORNING PRAYER

The will of God be done by us;
The law of God be kept by us;
Our evil will controlled by us;
Our sharp tongue checked by us;
Quick forgiveness offered by us;
Speedy repentance made by us;
Temptation sternly shunned by us;
Blessed death welcomed by us;
Angels' music heard by us;
God's highest praises sung by us.

KINDLING THE FIRE

This morning, as I kindle the fire upon my hearth, I pray that the flame of God's love may burn in my heart, and the hearts of all I meet today.

I pray that no envy and malice, no hatred or fear, may smother the flame.

I pray that indifference and apathy, contempt and pride, may not pour like cold water on the fire.

Instead, may the spark of God's love light the love in my heart, that it may burn brightly through the day.

And may I warm those that are lonely, whose hearts are cold and lifeless, so that all may know the comfort of God's love.

COVERING THE FIRE

Lord, preserve the fire, as Christ preserves us all.

Lord, may its warmth remain in our midst, as Christ is always among us.

Lord, may it rise to life in the morning, as we shall rise with Christ to eternal life.

"May we do the will of God… and rise in the light of heaven."

PATRICK'S EVENING HYMN

O Christ, Son of the living God,
May your holy angels guard our sleep.
May they watch us as we rest
And hover around our beds.

Let them reveal to us in our dreams
Visions of your glorious truth,
O High Prince of the universe,
O High Priest of the mysteries.

May no dreams disturb our rest
And no nightmares darken our dreams.
May no fears or worries delay
Our willing, prompt repose.

May the virtue of our daily work
Hallow our nightly prayers.
May our sleep be deep and soft,
So our work be fresh and hard.

GRACE BEFORE FOOD

*Dear Lord, bless this food for our use, and
us for your service.*

*May the food restore our strength, giving
new energy to tired limbs, new thought to
weary minds.*

*May the wine restore our souls, giving new
vision to dry spirits, new warmth to cold
hearts.*

*And once refreshed, we offer again our
minds and bodies, our hearts and spirits, to
proclaim your glory.*

A NIGHT PRAYER

May we do the will of God, sharing in
the death of Christ, and rise in the
light of heaven.

May we rest safely this night, sleep in
perfect peace, and rise with the
morning light.

May the Father watch over our beds,
Christ fill our dreams, and the
angels guard our souls.

◆4◆

ANIMALS *&* BIRDS

"Where birds of every kind of voice can grow up and find shelter."

THE HERMIT'S HUT

I wish, ancient and eternal King, to live
in a hidden hut in the wilderness.

A narrow blue stream beside it, and a
clear pool for washing away my sins
by the grace of the Holy Spirit.

A beautiful wood all around, where
birds of every kind of voice can
grow up and find shelter.

Facing southward to catch the sun,
with fertile soil around it suitable
for every kind of plant.

And virtuous young men to join me,
humble and eager to serve God.

Twelve young men – three fours, four
threes, two sixes, six pairs – willing
to do every kind of work.

A lovely church, with a white linen
cloth over the altar, a home for God
from heaven.

A Bible surrounded by four candles,
one for each of the gospels.

A special hut in which to gather for
meals, talking cheerfully as we eat,
without sarcasm, without boasting,
without any evil words.

Hens laying eggs for us to eat, leeks
growing near the stream, salmon
and trout to catch, and bees
providing honey.

Enough food and clothing given by
our Heavenly King, and enough
time to sit and pray to him.

A PEACEFUL COMPANY

I have a hut in the wood; no one knows of it except God.

An ash tree grows on one side, a hazel on the other, and a great oak tree overhangs it, sheltering it from wind and rain.

A honeysuckle climbs around its doorposts, and a blackbird nests in the roof, singing a sweet melody.

Around my hut are apple trees, yielding the richest fruit. Nearby is a spring, giving the purest water, and beside it watercress sprouts in abundance.

In the wood behind my hut swine, goats, boars, and deer graze peacefully together, with a family of badgers alongside them. And foxes come to leap among them. Yes, I have the most noble princes for company.

God has sent hens to lay eggs for me, and bees to give me honey. He has planted wild onions around me, and the trees are heavy with succulent berries.

Countless birds come to visit me: wild geese, ducks, before the beginning of winter; fair white birds, cranes, seagulls, singing the songs of the waves; the thrush chanting sweet carols, and in summer the familiar cuckoo above my hut.

All around me the most beautiful music plays: the songs of the birds, the lowing of cattle, the leaves rustling in the wind, the cascade of the river. No king could hire such music with gold; it is the music of Christ himself, given freely.

THE TREE OF LIFE

O, King of the Tree of Life,
The blossoms on the branches are
  your people,
The singing birds are your angels,
The whispering breeze is your Spirit.

O, King of the Tree of Life,
May the blossoms bring forth the
  sweetest fruit,
May the birds sing out the highest
  praise,
May your Spirit cover all with his
  gentle breath.

*"May the birds sing out
the highest praise."*

THE HERMIT AND
HIS BLACKBIRD

*I need to watch the sun, to calculate the
hours that I should pray to God. But the
blackbird who nests in the roof of my hut
makes no such calculations: he sings God's
praises all day long.*

*I need books to read, to learn the hidden
truths of God. But the blackbird who shares
my simple meals needs no written texts: he
can read the love of God in every leaf and
flower.*

*I need to beg forgiveness, to make myself
pure and fit for God. But the blackbird who
drinks with me from the stream sheds no
tears of contrition: he is as God made him,
with no stain of sin.*

THE SCHOLAR AND HIS CAT

I and my white cat each has his special
work: his mind is on hunting, while
mine is on the pursuit of truth.

To me, better than any worldly thing,
is to sit reading, penetrating the
mysteries of creation. My cat does
not envy me, but prefers his own
sport.

We are never bored at home, for we
each have endless enjoyment in our
own activities, exercising our skills
to the utmost.

Sometimes, after a desperate struggle,
he catches a mouse in his mouth; as
for me, I may catch some difficult
law, hard to comprehend, in my
mind.

He points his clear bright eye against
the wall from which the mice
emerge; I point my eye, feeble as
it is, against the great wall of
knowledge, from which truth
emerges.

He enjoys darting around, striving to
stick his claw into a mouse; I am
happy striving to grasp some
complex idea.

So long as we live in this way, neither
disturbs the other; each of us loves
his work, enjoying it all alone.

The task which he performs is the one
for which he was created; and I am
competent at my task, bringing
darkness to light.

An Untamed Horse

My heart is like an untamed horse.

For a while the horse is calm and
  steady,
Then suddenly it starts to buck.
For a while peace rules in my breast,
Then sinful desire overwhelms me.

A good rider can tame the horse,
So it always obeys commands.
The challenge of life is to tame the
· heart
So it always obeys the will.

The Little Gray Crow

The little gray crow with a bald head,
And the lark whose bed is the sky,
Must go where the fame of men
  must go,
And where men themselves must go.

All who have come, have gone,
All who now come, must go,
All who will come, shall go
To where the grace of God flows for ever.

Hunter and Hunted

I love hunting wild animals and birds.
I enjoy shooting an arrow in the air,
And watch my prey slump to the
  ground.
I love eating the meat I have killed.

But I hate being hunted by my enemies.
I fear the wild men with swords
  and cudgels;
And flee from those with lances
  and spears.
I dread seeing my friends fall in battle.

Should I do to birds and animals
What I hate being done to me?
Or should I treat God's creatures
As I want others to treat me?

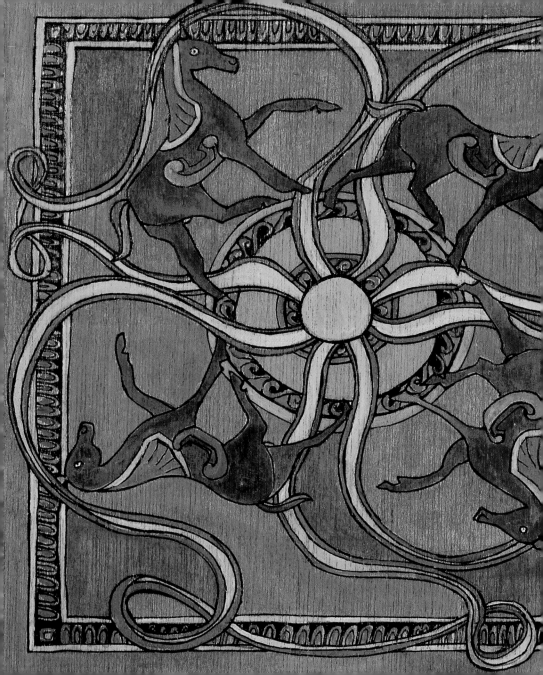

PART THREE

5

MIND & SOUL

*"My soul's desire is to imitate my King,
and to sing his praises always."*

THE SOUL'S DESIRE

My soul's desire is to see the face of
God, and to rest in his house.

My soul's desire is to study the
Scriptures, and to learn the ways of
God.

My soul's desire is to be freed from all
fear and sadness, and to share
Christ's risen life.

My soul's desire is to imitate my King,
and to sing his praises always.

My soul's desire is to enter the gates of
heaven, and to gaze upon the light
that shines for ever.

Dear Lord, you alone know what my
soul truly desires, and you alone can
satisfy those desires.

THE SOUL

*I am a flame of fire, blazing with passionate
love;*

*I am a spark of light, illuminating the
deepest truth;*

*I am a rough ocean, heaving with righteous
anger;*

*I am a calm lake, comforting the troubled
breast;*

I am a wild storm, raging at human sins;

*I am a gentle breeze, blowing hope in the
saddened heart;*

I am dry dust, choking worldly ambition;

I am wet earth, bearing rich fruits of grace.

CONFESSION

Jesus, forgive my sins.

Forgive the sins that I can remember, and also the sins I have forgotten.

Forgive the wrong actions I have committed, and the right actions I have omitted.

Forgive the times I have been weak in the face of temptation, and those when I have been stubborn in the face of correction.

Forgive the times I have been proud of my own achievements, and those when I have failed to boast of your works.

Forgive the harsh judgments I have made of others, and the leniency I have shown to myself.

Forgive the lies I have told to others, and the truths I have avoided.

Forgive me the pain I have caused others, and the indulgence I have shown to myself.

Jesus have pity on me, and make me whole.

THE ETERNAL WORDS

Fame may outlive a person's life.
A person's good works may be remembered
Long before his body has rotted.

Verses from a poet's poem
May outlast the verse of the poet
As the poems are very often repeated.

Listening longer than poems or verses
Is the book that speaks with undying tongue,
The Gospel of Christ.

Let me hear the words of that book
Today and tomorrow
And for all eternity.

*"Jesus have pity on me,
and make me whole."*

THE SCRIBE

My hand is weary from writing; my sharp quill is not steady; as its tender tip spits its dark, blue stream, the words which are formed on the page are jagged and uncertain.

O Lord, may it be your wisdom, not my folly, which passes through my arm and hand; may your words take shape upon the page. For when I am truly faithful to your dictation, my hand is firm and strong.

Let me never write words that are callous or profane; let your priceless jewels shine upon these pages.

'My thoughts can cross an ocean with a single leap.'

PRAYER FOR CONCENTRATION

God help my thoughts! They stray from me, setting off on the wildest journeys.

When I am in church, they run off like naughty children, quarreling, making trouble.

When I read the Bible, they fly to a distant city, filled with beautiful women.

My thoughts can cross an ocean with a single leap; they can fly from earth to heaven, and back again, in a single second.

They come to me for a fleeting moment, and then away they flee.

No chains, no locks can hold them back; no threats of punishment can restrain them, no hiss of a lash can frighten them.

They slip from my grasp like tails of eels; they swoop hither and thither like swallows in flight.

Dear, chaste, Christ, who can see into every heart and read every mind, take hold of my thoughts. Bring my thoughts back to me, and clasp me to yourself.

SELF-DECEPTION

To others I am always honest;
Myself I sometimes deceive.
To others I say what I believe to be
   true;
Myself I can make believe a lie.

To others my smile is intended to be
   sincere;
Myself I can fool into hiding my anger.
To others I always wish to do good;
Myself I can blind to my evil motives.
Lord, let me be as honest with myself
As I am with others.

SELF-KNOWLEDGE

Repentance requires honesty:
Honesty with oneself to acknowledge
   one's sins.
Honesty with God to confess one's sins.

Yet the commonest sin is lying:
Lying to oneself, ignoring one's sins,
Lying to others, for selfish ends.

If I am lying to myself
May God open my inward eyes to see,
And may I repent of every sin.

"My thoughts swirl like willow
branches caught in autumn winds."

A SOLDIER TO HIS GENERAL

When I come to you, Lord, to confess
  my sins.
Do I need to lie face down on the
  ground?
Should I grovel and abase myself
  before you?

You allowed wickedness into the
  world;
You gave me freedom to choose good
  and bad;
You let selfishness enter my breast.

The fight against sin is my life's work.
The war against sin gives meaning and
  energy.
Without sin I could not know
  goodness.

I come to God as a soldier to his
  general;
I ask him for stronger weapons in
  battle.
He inspires me to fight – my head is
  held high.

BRIGHTEN MY HEART

My body is as tense as a cat's
As it stalks its prey.
Lord, relax my body.

My thoughts swirl like willow branches
Caught in autumn winds.
Lord, still my thoughts.

My soul is as heavy as peat
Freshly dug from the bog.
Lord, lighten my soul.

My heart is as dark as soil
Sodden with the winter rains.
Lord, brighten my heart.

6

GUIDANCE & SAFETY

"Lord of my heart, give me vision to inspire me."

LORD OF MY HEART

Lord of my heart, give me vision to inspire me, that, working or resting, I may always think of you.

Lord of my heart, give me light to guide me, that, at home or abroad, I may always walk in your way.

Lord of my heart, give me wisdom to direct me, that, thinking or acting, I may always discern right from wrong.

Lord of my heart, give me courage to strengthen me, that, among friends or enemies, I may always proclaim your justice.

Lord of my heart, give me trust to console me, that, hungry or well-fed, I may always rely on your mercy.

Lord of my heart, save me from empty praise, that I may always boast of you.

Lord of my heart, save me from worldly wealth, that I may always look to the riches of heaven.

Lord of my heart, save me from military prowess, that I may always seek your protection.

Lord of my heart, save me from vain knowledge, that I may always study your word.

Lord of my heart, save me from unnatural pleasures, that I may always find joy in your wonderful creation.

Heart of my own heart, whatever may befall me, rule over my thoughts and feelings, my words and actions.

St. Patrick's Breastplate

I gird myself today with the might of
  heaven:
The rays of the sun,
The beams of the moon,
The glory of fire,
The speed of wind,
The depth of sea,
The stability of earth,
The hardness of rock.

I gird myself today with the power of God:
God's strength to comfort me,
God's might to uphold me,
God's wisdom to guide me,
God's eye to look before me,
God's ear to hear me,
God's word to speak for me,
God's hand to lead me,
God's way to lie before me,
God's shield to protect me,
God's angels to save me
From the snares of the Devil,
From temptations to sin,
From all who wish me ill,
Both far and near,
Alone and with others.

May Christ guard me today
From poison and fire,
From drowning and wounding,
So my mission may bear
Fruit in abundance.
Christ behind and before me,
Christ beneath and above me,
Christ with me and in me,
Christ around and about me,
Christ on my left and my right,
Christ when I rise in the morning,
Christ when I lie down at night,
Christ in each heart that thinks of me,
Christ in each mouth that speaks of me,
Christ in each eye that sees me,
Christ in each ear that hears me.

I arise today
Through the power of the Trinity,
Through faith in the threeness,
Through trust in the oneness,
Of the Maker of earth,
And the Maker of heaven.

"I gird myself today with the
might of heaven."

47

GOD'S FLOCK

When you go out on the hills
   to tend your flock,
You ask yourself daily: "Have any
   gone astray?"
So you count your sheep one by one;
And if any are missing, you start to search.

We are God's flock, and the hills
   are his world,
He asks himself daily: "Have any
   gone astray?"
So he counts his sheep one by one;
And if any are missing, he starts
   to search.

When winter comes, you round up
   your sheep,
And you and your dogs lead
   them to shelter.
It's too late to search,
The wandering sheep die on the hills.

When death comes, God rounds up
   his sheep,
And he and his angels lead
   them to heaven.
It's then too late to search,
The wandering sheep die in hell.

We know when winter is coming,
But death may come at any time.
So do not wander from God's flock,
Lest you're away when
   the searching stops.

GOD'S WILL

Anyone who rejects God's will
Is like a leaking ship on a stormy sea,
Is like an eagle caught in a trap,
Is like an apple tree which never blossoms.

Anyone who obeys God's will
Is like the golden rays of the summer sun,
Is like a silver chalice overflowing with wine,
Is like a beautiful bride ready for love.

DANGER OF DEATH

When I go out alone on the mountain,
O King of roads, may my journey
be safe. Death is no nearer to me on
the mountain peak, than if I were
guarded by three thousand men.

Even if I had three thousand young
men with armor of the thickest
hide, when the call of death comes
there is no fortress that could hold
out against it.

Even if I had no protection whatever,
there is no snare that could trap me
if death was not calling.

If someone tries to ambush me and
steal my goods, he will not succeed
unless the Lord allows it.

No mere human being can shorten my
life, unless it is shortened by the
King who shaped the earth and
sends the seasons.

I ignore all omens that people say
bring ill luck, because God alone
determines our fortunes and
misfortunes.

The warrior whose clean white flesh is
cut open with a sword need have no
greater fear of death than a man
who cowers at home.

Everyone has only one day of real
danger, and that is the day on which
he dies.

So I have no fear of earthly dangers; I
fear God alone – and him do I trust.

*"Anyone who rejects God's will is like a
leaking ship on a stormy sea."*

PART FOUR

7

WEALTH *&* POVERTY

"I should welcome the poor to my feast,
for they are God's children."

BRIGID'S FEAST

I should like a great lake of finest ale
For the King of kings.
I should like a table of the choicest food
For the family of heaven.
Let the ale be made from the fruits of faith,
And the food be forgiving love.

I should welcome the poor to my feast,
For they are God's children.
I should welcome the sick to my feast,
For they are God's joy.
Let the poor sit with Jesus at the
  highest place,
And the sick dance with the angels.

God bless the poor,
God bless the sick,
And bless our human race.

God bless our food,
God bless our drink,
All homes, O God, embrace.

THE RICH MAN'S SOUL

Let me take you inside the soul of a rich
  man without love, and a wealthy man
  without friends.

The darkest night, with neither moon nor
  stars, is like the brightest day compared
  with the darkness of this soul.

The coldest winter, with thick snow and
  hard ice, is like the warmest summer
  compared with the coldness of this soul.

The bleakest mountain, bare and swept by
  gales, is like the lushest meadow
  compared with the bleakness of this soul.

You would rather have your body hacked in
  pieces than present such a soul as this;
  you would rather be boiled or burned
  alive than suffer such inward torment.

THE RICH MAN'S FRIENDS

Among the sleek and wealthy, the poor
are regarded as fools.

Once I was wealthy, and flocks of
friends thronged to my door; I grew
poor, and none came near.

In summer people wanted to walk in
my shadow; now as I pass in my
coarse tunic they avoid me.

*"Let my love for others
be God's love."*

The person they saw when I was rich
was not me, but my wealth; now
they see nobody, pretending I no
longer exist.

If I were rich again, their eyes would
brighten as they saw me, and their
arms reach out to embrace me; now
they can watch me collapse without
lifting a hand to help me.

The world jibes at me because my
barns are bare and my hut empty;
the proud peer down their noses at
me, the rich curl their lips.

O Lord, let everyone know both
wealth and poverty in their lives;
then all will be happy to share what
they have.

REMEMBER THE POOR

Remember the poor when you look
out on fields you own, on your plump
cows grazing.

Remember the poor when you look
into your barn, at the abundance of
your harvest.

Remember the poor when the wind
howls and the rain falls, as you sit
warm and dry in your house.

Remember the poor when you eat
fine meat and drink fine ale, at your
fine carved table.

The cows have grass to eat, the rabbits
have burrows for shelter, the birds have
warm nests.

But the poor have no food except
what you feed them, no shelter except
your house when you welcome them,
no warmth except your glowing fire.

WEALTH AS LOAN

When I give alms to the poor,
Let me not congratulate myself,
Let there be no pride in my act.

The wealth I possess is on loan;
God has made me its steward.
I am his hands and his heart.

Let my love for others be God's love;
Let my pity for the needy be his;
Let my alms be received as his gift.

◆ 8 ◆

LIFE & DEATH

"Wait for me, Mary's Son, until I am old,
wise from the passing of years."

Wait for me, King of Heaven, until I am pure, fit to live in your house.

Wait for me, Mary's Son, until I am old, wise from the passing of years.

When a young boy is carried off before his years of playing are over, no one knows what greatness he has missed; only in adulthood comes the full bloom of our gifts.

A calf should not be killed before it is full-grown, nor a pig slaughtered when it is still sucking at the sow's breast.

A bough should not be cut until it has flowered, nor a field harvested until the grain is full.

The sun should not set at midday, nor rise at midnight.

Keep my soul here on earth, for it is like soft, unformed clay, not ready to be received by you.

Yet even if you cut me off in my youth, I shall not complain, but continue to worship you.

YOUTH AND AGE

Once my hair was shining yellow,
    falling in long ringlets round my
    brow; now it is gray and sparse, all
    luster gone.

Once as I walked along the lane, girls'
    heads would turn to look at me;
    now no woman looks my way, no
    heart races as I approach.

Once my body was filled with desire,
    and I had energy to satisfy my every
    want; now desire has grown dim, I
    have no energy to satisfy even the
    few desires that remain.

Yet I would rather chilly age than hot
    youth; I would rather know that
    God is near, than have no thought
    of him in my head.

I have had my day on earth; now I
    look to eternity in heaven.

THE DYING HERMIT

*Alone in my little hut in the forest I have
prepared for my death; without moving I
have been on a long journey toward my
heavenly home.*

*I have trodden down my evil passions,
stamped upon anger and greed; I have cast
aside jealousy and fear, leaving them by the
wayside.*

*At times my pace has been bold and fast
along the gospel way; at times I have
crawled on bended knee, crying for
forgiveness.*

*Now my journey is almost finished, my
Creator comes to fetch me; alone I came to
my hut in the forest, alone in death I shall
leave it.*

"Now my journey is almost finished, my Creator comes to fetch me."

FINAL REFLECTIONS

I give you thanks, my King, for the care you have lavished upon me.

I have for six months been lying on my bed, my body racked by disease; I am a prisoner, held in chains by my illness.

My strength is gone, from my head to my feet I can barely move; my weakness is like fetters holding me down.

I am like a blind man unable to see the world around me; for six months I have seen only the walls of my hut.

You have nailed me to my cross; this sickness is my crucifixion.

And so I give you thanks, my King, for bringing me joyfully to judgment.

Tomorrow I shall die, and see you face to face; tomorrow your lash on my body shall cease, and I shall be at peace.

If now my body is shrouded by clouds of darkness, my soul basks in warm light; if now my eyes are filled with bitter tears, my soul can taste the sweetest honey.

I am like a mouse, caught in a trap and shaken in the claws of a cat; tomorrow I shall be as free as the wind.

My present pains are as nothing compared to the enormity of my sin; your mercy is infinite and eternal.

DYING DAY

When your eyes are closing and your mouth opening, may God bring you comfort on that day.

When your senses are fading and your limbs growing cold, may God save your soul on that day.

Pray to heaven and to all the angels, pray to heaven and to all the saints, that God will pour out his mercy on that day.

Pray that the Virgin will reach out and embrace you, that Michael will reach down and lift you up, on the day of your death.

REMEMBER YOUR END

Remember, O friend, your end.

Now you are strong and fit, filled with ambition, boasting of your achievements; but all your success is a mere passing shadow.

Remember you are made of clay, and to clay you will return.

Now you are healthy and handsome, filled with energy, proud of your work; but all your joys are mere passing shadows.

Remember your life is the breath of God, which at death will depart.

Now your life on earth is solid and stable; but soon it will dissolve, your body crumbling to dust.

Remember, O friend, your end.

BIBLIOGRAPHY

This is a list of primary sources concerning Celtic Christianity.

Anderson, A.O and M.O., *Adomnan's Life of St. Columba*, London, 1961.

Bieler, L., *The Patrician Texts in the Book of Armagh*, Dublin, 1979.

Carmichael, A., *Carmina Gadelica*, 2 vols, Edinburgh, 1928.

Clough, S.D.P., *A Gaelic Anthology*, Dublin, 1987.

Colgrave, R., *Two Lives of St. Cuthbert*, Cambridge, 1940.

Doble, G.H., *Lives of the Welsh Saints*, Cardiff, 1971.

Flower, R.E.W., *Poems and Translations*, London, 1931.

Forbes, A.P., *Lives of St. Ninian and St. Kentigern*, Edinburgh, 1874.

Graves, A.P., *A Celtic Psaltery*, London, 1917.

Greene, D. and O'Connor, F., *A Golden Treasury of Irish Poetry 600 to 1200 AD*, London, 1967.

Hull, E., *The Poem-Book of the Gael*, London, 1912.

Hyde, D., *The Religious Songs of Connacht*, 2 vols, Dublin, 1906.

Jackson, K., *Studies in Early Celtic Poetry*, Cambridge, 1935.

McLean, G.R.D., *Poems of the Western Highlanders*, London, 1961.

Metcalfe, W.M., *Lives of Scottish Saints*, 2 vols, Paisley, 1899.

Meyer, K., *Selections from Ancient Irish Poetry*, London, 1911.

Murphy, G., *Early Irish Lyrics*, Oxford, 1956.

O'Donoghue, D., *St. Brendan the Voyager*, Dublin, 1895.

Rees, W.J., *Lives of the Cambro British Saints*, Llandovery, 1853.

Sharp, E., *Lyra Celtica*, Edinburgh, 1896.

Stevens, J., *Bede's Ecclesiastical History of the English Nation*, London, 1910.

Stokes, W., *Lives of Saints from the Book of Lismore*, Oxford, 1890.

Webb, J.F., *Lives of the Saints*, London, 1965.

Patrick on the shores of Ireland in the middle of the fifth century.

Possibly some of the prayers were composed to the great Celtic saints whose names still excite the Christian soul: Patrick himself, Brigid, Columba, Kevin, Mungo, Aidan, David, Cuthbert, Piran, and the rest. But most were probably first used by hermits and evangelists, and by chieftains and peasants, whose names have long been forgotten. The important point is that none of them is mere empty piety; in each one the emotions and experiences of daily life are offered to God. This is the reason why prayers formulated so long ago can be our prayers today.

Celtic Christianity existed in full bloom for two or three centuries and then began to fade, overwhelmed by colder spiritual forces. Yet since that time Christians have consistently rediscovered it and been inspired

The great flowering of Celtic Christianity began in the fifth century.

afresh by its beauty. Happily, this is happening again. People are wanting to bring religion out into the open, so that it can inform and sanctify every aspect of human existence; they find within Celtic spirituality the means of doing this. These prayers are for everyone who wants to live their faith every minute of every day of every week of every year.

PART ONE

◆ 1 ◆

EARTH & HEAVEN

*"Heaven is like an open window, in which
all can move freely."*